–LINES TO LIVE BY–

TAYLOR SWIFT

VOLUME II

POP PRESS

Pop Press, an imprint of Ebury Publishing
20 Vauxhall Bridge Road
London SW1V 2SA

Pop Press is part of the Penguin Random House group of companies
whose addresses can be found at global.penguinrandomhouse.com

First published by Pop Press in 2024

www.penguin.co.uk

A CIP catalogue record for this book is available from the British Library

ISBN: 9781529945645

Typeset in 12/15pt ElegantGaramond BT by Jouve (UK), Milton Keynes
Printed and bound in Great Britain by Clays Ltd, Elcograf S.p.A.

The authorised representative in the EEA is Penguin Random House
Ireland, Morrison Chambers, 32 Nassau Street, Dublin D02 YH68

CONTENTS

INTRODUCTION 1

BE ROMANTIC. 13

BE EMOTIONAL. 25

BE MATURE 37

BE PASSIONATE 47

BE EMPOWERED 57

BE REBELLIOUS 67

BE JOYFUL. 77

BE THOUGHTFUL. 89

BE REFLECTIVE 99

BE CREATIVE. 109

INTRODUCTION

Songwriter. Philosopher. People-watcher. Lover. Daughter. Film maker. Friend.

Taylor Swift, who released her first album at the age of 16 and shot to international stardom, is now the single most successful woman in the global music business and here's why; she's a great storyteller, she's stayed true to herself, and those stories are the stories of not only her life but also ours.

Since 2006, we've seen Taylor grow from a tousled-haired, eager-to-please Nashville teen to a polished entrepreneur and entertainer who is still strumming her 12-string country guitar and telling it like it is; and whose recent Eras tour has finally made her a billionaire.

There are now 10 different college courses devoted to the 'study' of Taylor Swift with one professor even likening the songstress and her storytelling talent to the poet William Wordsworth.

We've laughed with her, cried with her, loved with her, and lost with her; and with each new chapter of her life, we've been inspired – like her – to reinvent ourselves for the adventures ahead and, most of all, to just keep going whatever life throws our way.

Taylor learned early on to master and relish the art of reinvention. She started out in country but soon crossed to pop stardom and in later albums, she's rocking the folk vibe. So, as well as teaching fans that they too can reinvent themselves whenever and however they want, we've all come to love the fact that whenever there's a new TS album, there's also a new life lesson. And in this book, we look backwards and forwards at what Taylor has learned – and shared – along the way.

THE ALBUMS AND THEIR LIFE LESSONS

Album: Taylor Swift

Release: 2006

An album that captures the giddy heights and crashing lows of early teenage love and romance.

Life lesson: Be Romantic

What Taylor said: 'When I was a teenager and writing about my troubles in High School all the drama, and the pining away ... that was all so valid to me at that time in my life.'

Album: Fearless

Release: 2008

An album that captures all the emotions, from the highest highs to the lowest of lows.

Life lesson: Be Emotional

What Taylor said: 'It's fearless to have faith that someday things will change.'

Album: Speak Now

Release: 2010

An album that captures the rollercoaster of a songwriter starting to find her voice at the end of her teens.

Life lesson: Be Mature

What Taylor said: 'It was an album that was the most precious to me because of its vast extremes. It was unfiltered and potent.'

Album: Red

Release: 2012

An album that captures the last time the songstress is still naïve enough to be taken by surprise when a major but tumultuous love affair dies.

Life lesson: Be Passionate

What Taylor said: 'I was 22 when this album was first released and some of it is really sad because that's the stuff I had been going through. It was nice when we rerecorded it not to have to take breaks between interviews to cry.'

Album: 1989

Release: 2014

An album that captures the spirit of optimism and the world as your oyster.

Life lesson: Be Empowered

What Taylor said: 'The connection I feel to fans and the connection I feel to all the people I write songs about is what makes me feel like my life has a purpose.'

Album: Reputation

Release: 2017

An album that captures the frustrations of being a female breaking out of 'the good little girl programmes' to find her voice.

Life lesson: Be Rebellious

What Taylor said: '[Reputation is] a goth-punk moment of female rage at being gaslit by an entire social structure.'

Album: Lover

Release: 2019

An album that captures the joy of two people being the last on the dancefloor at 3am.

Life lesson: Be Joyful

What Taylor said: 'With this album, I felt like I sort of gave myself permission to revisit older themes that I used to write about, maybe look at them with fresh eyes.'

Albums: Folklore/Evermore

Release: 2020/2020

Both albums are a Masterclass in what it means to be human and in love or heartbroken but with these albums Taylor broke away from being a diarist songwriter to writing about fictional characters.

Life lesson: Be Thoughtful

What Taylor said: 'With Evermore I had this feeling of quiet conclusion and closure. We did what we set out to do.'

Album: Midnights

Release: 2022

An album that let Taylor celebrate all of the highpoints and reflect on the struggles she has been through as an artist and a person.

Life lesson: Be Reflective

What Taylor said: 'One of the themes of Midnights is how you're feeling in the middle of the night, and that can be intense self-hatred, intense self-love – you go through these very polarising emotions when you're up late at night and your brain just spirals.'

Album: The Tortured Poets Department

Release: 2024

An album that, according to *Variety*, comes the closest of any of her original albums to 'just drilling a tube directly into her brain and letting listeners mainline what comes out'.

Life lesson: Be Creative

What Taylor said: 'I've never had an album where I needed songwriting more than I needed it on Tortured Poets.'

BE
ROMANTIC

Who doesn't like the excitement of butterflies in the tummy, a racing heartbeat, and a silly giddiness when you catch sight of or have any kind of contact with the one you love. Defined as 'that feeling of mystery and excitement linked to love', it's no wonder Taylor has had hit after hit with albums that celebrate, explore, dissect, and mourn the one thing we all yearn for and spend lifetimes seeking — namely that wonderful feeling of romantic love, which can hit anyone at any time, and often arrives when you least expect it.

'I don't think there's an option for me to fall in love slowly, or at medium speed. I either do or I don't.'

'You can't predict love or plan for it. For someone like me who is obsessed with organisation and planning, I love the idea that love is the one exception to that. Love is the one wild card.'

'As soon as I wrote the song, I knew "Fearless" would be the title track for the *Fearless* album. It was about fearlessly falling in love and not caring if you're going to get hurt.'

'I know it sounds cliché,
but she's good to talk
to about boys. She knows
her stuff.'

– Florence Welch

'I realised there's this idea
of happily ever after which
in real life doesn't happen.'

'When we're falling in love or out of it, that's when we most need a song that says how we feel.'

'Every person I've fallen for, they've all been a song. Songs I'm proud of. That kind of justifies them being in my life.'

BE
EMOTIONAL

An emotion is a (usually) strong internal feeling that is triggered by an external event – good or bad. It may be happiness, sorrow, joy, or anger that emerges as a feeling that rises up from the pit of the stomach up to hijack the rest of your day. But the truth is, emotions are a good thing. They tell that you are very much still alive and still care, one way or the other. Blocked emotions – those you can't find any way of expressing or are too scared to show – will always get their moment in the spotlight. You may think they are dead and buried but just ask Taylor who knows, more than most, the best way to process emotions, especially the tricky ones, is to find a way to share them. A feeling that you talk about is a feeling that soon loses its power over you.

'Over the years I've learned that anger can manifest itself in a lot of different ways, but the healthiest way it can manifest itself in my life is when I can write a song about it.'

'Taylor and I first met at an awards show. The atmosphere at those is not the coolest and a lot of people behave like garbage, so it is easy to spot a great person. She was so cool and wonderful and warm.'

– Jack Antonoff

'I know I'm going on that
stage whether I'm sick,
injured, heartbroken,
uncomfortable, or stressed.
That's part of my identity as
a human being now.'

'I want to remember the colour of the sweater, the temperature of the air, the creak of the floorboards, the time on the clock when your heart was stolen or shattered or healed or claimed forever.'

'Every time I sing "White Horse" which is all about comparing the fairy tale we are taught as kids with what can happen with young love and young heartbreak, I get emotional.'

'Taylor told me you must sing about what's happening in your life.'

– Florence Welch

'A lot of the time when we lose things, we gain things too.'

BE
MATURE

Think about what makes a person seem mature. Do they knee-jerk react to every slight or criticism – perceived or real. Or do they take a moment to check in with themselves and see things from another person's point of view? Compassion is a sign of maturity. So is the ability to recognise when a relationship has had its moment in the sun. Putting boundaries in place and saying no to toxic 'love' is another sign of maturity. So is trusting that little voice in your head that tells you when you run towards someone and when to run away. Maturity has nothing to do with biological age and everything to do with knowing what really matters and trusting yourself.

'Having the world treat my love life like a spectator sport in which I lose every single game was not a great way to date in my teens and twenties, but it taught me to protect my private life fiercely.'

'With *Folklore*, one of the main themes was conflict resolution. Figuring out how to get through something with someone.'

'*Evermore* deals a lot with endings. All the kinds of ways we can end something [. . .] and the pain that goes along with that.'

'When I'm 40 and nobody wants to see me in a sparkly dress anymore, I'll be, like: "Cool, I'll just go in the studio and write songs for kids." It's looking like a good pension plan.'

'Everything is an ongoing
storyline and you're
always battling the
complexities of life.'

'It happens to women so often that, as we get older and see how the world works, we're able to see through what is gaslighting.'

BE
PASSIONATE

You know that meme that says, 'dance like nobody is watching'? That's an invitation to unleash the passion bubbling just under the surface and show the world who you really are. Unapologetically. Don't shrink-wrap yourself for anyone. If you feel passionately (strongly) about something, give yourself permission to say so. If you love someone deeply, tell them. If you care about fighting animal cruelty, supporting LGBTQ+ communities, or protecting women at risk of violence, then find your voice – like Taylor – and find a way to say so. Others may not agree but they will always respect your commitment and willingness to put yourself out there and tell it like it is – in love and in life.

'I don't seem to have any
real strategy or pattern
when it comes to love . . .
At times I've been really
guarded and careful and
afraid to trust someone. But
other times, you want to
jump in headfirst.'

'My friendship with Taylor is one of my deep friendships. [. . .] She's a real superpower and I love and admire her so much.'

– Laura Dern

'It's all about walking a tightrope between not being so fragile and breakable that they can level you with one blow and being raw enough to feel it and write about it when you feel it.'

'I'd so much rather feel everything than end up the typical Hollywood sad cliché of the poor lonely starlet with no one because she put up all these walls and didn't trust anyone.'

'Taylor's an extremely hard worker, and I'm sure she's got giant goals. But it's not *all* about ambition: it's about passion and committing yourself to your passion.'

– Shania Twain

'I'd rather be with someone who has his own voice and passion and ambition.'

BE
EMPOWERED

We all stand on the shoulders of the trailblazers who have come before us, but real empowerment is a thing that unfolds inside you, not outside. Taylor learned this the hard way when, in 2016, her world was rocked by multiple missiles of criticism coming from so many quarters she had no choice but to look inside herself. What had happened that had turned her from the cute lanky 'Sweet Sixteen' kid with the bouncy curls who'd just happened to have some mega hits? Why were so many people suddenly being so mean? What had happened, in short, is that cute Taylor was growing up into Taylor who meant business and wasn't afraid to stand her ground. In other words, Taylor was on her way to the impressive and empowered woman we see today.

'I didn't want to just be another girl singer recording other people's songs. I wanted there to be something that set me apart. And I knew that had to be my writing.'

'It's important to be confident in who you are, because the best thing you can bring to a relationship is a whole person.'

'Be discerning. If someone in your life is hurting you, draining you, or causing you pain in a way that feels unresolvable, blocking their number isn't cruel.'

'My response to anything
that happens, good or bad,
is to keep making things.
Keep making art. There's
no point trying to defeat
your enemies. Happily,
trash takes itself out
every single time.'

'She's a brilliant songwriter which is a title given to a lot of people when very few of them are. [. . .] She doesn't need anyone to write a great song.'

– Jack Antonoff

'The female artists I know of have to remake themselves like 20 times more than the male artists, or you're out of a job.'

BE
REBELLIOUS

There's little point in being a rebel without a cause but if you see or feel injustice or know that something needs to change, then you'll need to channel Taylor's rebellious streak and put your neck on the line. One of the best examples of this was her decision to re-record her original albums after her record label refused, time and again, to allow Taylor to buy the rights to her back catalogue to own the body of work she had created. That took guts to show a rebellious side and was seen as a risky move – until Swiftie fans got on board with her message that the person who knows a song best is the person who wrote it, and favoured the Taylor Versions of her albums over the originals.

'There's this weird theme running through the video for the song "Anti-Hero" where I bleed glitter. It's sort of a metaphor for how I don't feel like a normal person.'

'There's always some
standard of beauty that
you're not meeting.'

'As far as the need to rebel against the idea of you or the image of you: Like, I feel no need to burn down the house I built by hand. I can make additions to it. I can redecorate. But I built this.'

'I would describe myself
as a rebel in some ways,
but not in others.'

'**You are not** the opinion of somebody who doesn't know you. **You are not** damaged goods just because you made mistakes in your life.'

BE
JOYFUL

Taylor's best friend is her mother, Andrea, who named Taylor after James Taylor the singer/songwriter. Taylor Swift has said that she never needed to go to therapy because she talks to her mom, who goes on tour with her, every single day and about everything. Both Taylor and Andrea, a two-time breast cancer survivor, learned from experience that none of us know what lies around the corner tomorrow or the day after, and so given the choice, why not be joyful and celebrate the wins – large and small. It is not the easiest of the life lessons, but it is probably the single most important one.

'Every day I try to remind myself of the good in the world, the love I've witnessed, and the faith I have in humanity. We have to live bravely in order to truly feel alive, and that means not being ruled by our greatest fears.'

'I have this really high priority on happiness and finding something to be happy about. My ultimate goal is to end up being happy, most of the time.'

'That's my sis. She's so funny.'

– Ice Spice (2023)

'I've just never been this happy in my life in all aspects of my life, ever.'

'She's so great! We're very different, but she has such a sick sense of humor.'

– Emma Stone

'Somehow, she's even better in real life.'

– Blake Lively

'Don't base your day
and your happiness on
social media.'

BE
THOUGHTFUL

Thinking about how and why we respond in certain ways to particular people and the things that happen to us helps us to not only get to know ourselves better but also other people too. And that, in turn, will improve all our relationships. When you track Taylor's career through her interviews and the things she has said in public, you can clearly see one of her biggest life lessons has been learning to take a pause, slow down, and really think about what she is saying and what it all means. She's still enthusiastic, just more thoughtful with it.

'The characteristic of a great friend is sincerity. My friends are all really different but the thing they all have in common is sincerity. We're never going to turn in each other. We don't gossip about each other, it's a kind of alliance.'

'Anything can change so you just have to appreciate the fact that you get to do what you love one more day. And that keeps you in perspective.'

'No matter what happens in
life, be good to people.
Being good to people is
a wonderful legacy to
leave behind.'

'I think these days, people are reaching out for connection and comfort in the music they listen to.'

'What I worry about is that
I never want to end up kind
of a self-centred, vain
human being.'

'I just sort of feel like my life finally feels like it makes sense.'

BE
REFLECTIVE

Most creatives will tell you when they finally sit down to paint, sculpt, or write a song, the hard work has already been done because whilst they've been busy doing other things, their mind has been sifting through events, experiences, feelings, ideas, and even dreams, and reflecting on what's happened and how it made them feel or see things in a new way. Reflection takes time and cannot be rushed, and you can see how Taylor has shifted her songwriting from reaction to reflection. It is a sign of maturity and one of the gifts of becoming older and wiser.

'Some people get freaked
out by huge displays of
emotion from fans, but
I like criers and people
who come up to me
bawling and screaming.'

'It's very brave to be vulnerable about your feelings in any sense, in any situation. But it's even more brave to be honest about your feelings and who you love when you know that that might be met with adversity from society.'

'I've been raised up and down the flagpole of public opinion so many times in the last 20 years [. . .] I've been given a tiara, then had it taken away.'

'May we end up in a world
where everyone can live
and love equally, and no
one has to be afraid to be
vulnerable and say
how they feel.'

'I think it's healthy for everyone to go a few years without dating, just because you need to get to know who you are.'

BE
CREATIVE

You are unique. There is only one person like you. There has never been a person the same as you until now and there will never be anyone the same again. It is this uniqueness that lies at the heart of our need to create because it is this uniqueness that is yearning to be expressed. You can dance, you can journal, you can cook, or you can take a pottery class. You can tie yourself up in knots making a macramé moon catcher or dig out your grandma's knitting patterns and make a beanie. Whatever it is you decide to create, put your whole soul and your whole self into it. There is nothing more nourishing, sustaining, or rewarding than finding a creative way to tell the world (and maybe even yourself when you are feeling low) just who you really are. Ask Taylor – she's made a superstar career of it!

'I try really hard to be a nice
person but if you break my
heart or hurt my feelings
or are really mean to me,
I'm gonna write a
song about you.'

'I wrote my first hit "Tim McGraw" about this guy I was dating who was about to go off to college, so I knew we were going to break up. So, I wanted to write about all the things that would remind him of me.'

'"Teardrops on my Guitar" was about a guy I had a huge crush on at school, but he never knew it. So really it is about hiding your feelings.'

'I love having a goal, feeling like I'm on a mission. I love trying to beat what I've done so far.'

'What's cool about Taylor is that when she's being artistic and creating, she's not a superstar. She's like a 15-year-old in a room with a guitar, writing.'

– Jack Antonoff

'You don't have to be in love or be in a relationship to write about it. And you don't have to have a boyfriend or have broken up to write about it. In fact, don't have successful relationships – they're no fun to write about.'

'Daydreaming was kind of my number one thing when I was little, because I didn't have much of a social life going on.'

ACKNOWLEDGEMENTS

Page 5 from Apple Music, 'Taylor Swift's Songwriting Process on 'evermore'' (Zane Lowe, 2021). Page 5 from People, 'Everything Taylor Swift Has Ever Said About Heartbreak and Moving On' (Laura Cohen, 2016). Page 6 from Billboard, 'Taylor Swift Reveals the 'Saddest,' 'Most Scathing' & 'Most Wistfully Romantic' Songs She's Ever Written' (Rania Aniftos, 2023). Page 7 from Entertainment Weekly, 'Taylor Swift delivers the 'biggest burn' when asked about the people she's written songs about' (Nick Romano, 2021). Page 7 from Centre for Optimism, 'Taylor Swift: Magnetic Optimism and Joy' (Victor Perton, 2019). Page 8 from Time Magazine, '2023 Person of the Year' (Sam Lansky, 2023). Page 8 from The New York Times, 'Taylor Swift Tells Us How She Wrote 'Lover'' (2019). Page 9 from Apple Music, 'Taylor Swift's Songwriting Process on 'evermore'' (Zane Lowe, 2021). Page 9-10 from Genius.com, 'Karma: What have the artists said about the song?' (2022). Page 10 from BBC News, 'Taylor Swift Tortured Poets Department review' (Mark Savage, 2024). Page 16 from Parade Magazine, 'Taylor Swift Parade Magazine Interview: Singer Reveals She Wants a 'Bad Boy' (Stephen L Betts, 2012). Page 17 from Glamour.com, 'Taylor Swift Talks' (Laurie Sandell, 2010). Page 18 from Audacy Music, 'Taylor Swift on which songs made her emotional while re-recording 'Fearless'' (2021). Page 19 from Cosmopolitan, 'Revisiting Taylor Swift and Florence Welch's Friendship Amid Their 'The Tortured Poets Department' Collab' (Samantha Olson, 2024). Page 20 from Elle,

'Taylor Swift Has No Regrets' (Tavi Gevinson, 2015). Page 21 from The Guardian, 'I want to believe in pretty lies' (Alex Macpherson, 2012). Page 22 from MTV, 'Taylor Swift Opens Up About Marriage And Kids' (Jocelyn Vena, 2010). Page 28 from Teen Vogue, 'Taylor Swift Tortured Poets Department 5 Stages of Grief Theory, Explained' (P. Claire Dodson, 2024). Page 29 from Cosmopolitan, 'All the sweet details of Taylor Swift and Jack Antonoff's friendship' (Mehera Bonner, 2024). Page 30 from Time Magazine, '2023 Person of the Year' (Sam Lansky, 2023). Page 31 from Elle, 'For Taylor Swift, Pop Is Personal' Taylor Swift, 2019). Page 32 from Audacy Music, 'Taylor Swift on which songs made her emotional while re-recording 'Fearless'' (2021). Page 33 from Cosmopolitan, 'Revisiting Taylor Swift and Florence Welch's Friendship Amid Their 'The Tortured Poets Department' Collab' (Samantha Olson, 2024). Page 34 from Teen Vogue, 'Taylor Swift Tortured Poets Department 5 Stages of Grief Theory, Explained' (P. Claire Dodson, 2024). Page 40 from Hola, 'Taylor Swift Talks About The Public Obsession With Her Love Life In NYU Commencement Speech' (Jovita Trujillo, 2022). Page 41 from from Apple Music, 'Taylor Swift's Songwriting Process on 'evermore'' (Zane Lowe, 2021). Page 42 from Apple Music, 'Taylor Swift's Songwriting Process on 'evermore'' (Zane Lowe, 2021). Page 43 from, 'Why Taylor Swift Is the Reigning Queen of Pop' (Jody Rosen, 2013). Page 44 from The Guardian, 'I want to believe in pretty lies' (Alex Macpherson, 2012). Page 45 from The Guardian, 'Taylor Swift: I was literally about to break' (Laura Snapes, 2019). Page 50 from Glamour.com, 'Taylor Swift Talks' (Laurie Sandell, 2010). Page 51 from People, 'Laura Dern Reveals 'Deep Friendship' with Taylor Swift' (Scott Huver, 2024). Page 52 from Esquire, 'The ESQ&A: Taylor Swift' (Scott Raab, 2014). Page 53 from Marie Claire, 'Taylor Swift: I Started Writing Songs Because I Had No Friends' (Lisa Potter, 2013). Page 54 from People, 'Shania

Twain Praises Taylor Swift's 'Passion' and Work Ethic' (Jack Irvin, 2024). Page 55 from Glamour, 'Taylor Swift: Bomb-Shell in Blue Jeans' (Laurie Sandell, 2009). Page 60 from Udiscovermusic, 'How Taylor Swift's Debut Album Set Her Apart From The Rest' (Martin Chilton, 2023). Page 61 from The Boot, 'Taylor Swift Talks Friends, Fears and Fairy Tales' (Melinda Newman, 2008). Page 62 from Popsugar, 'Taylor Swift Shares All the Lessons She Has Learned Before Turning 30, and I'm Taking Notes' (Kelsie Gibson, 2019). Page 63 from Inc, 'With 7 Short Words, Taylor Swift Just Taught a Brilliant Lesson in Emotional Intelligence' (Bill Murphy, 2023). Page 64 from Paths of Our Child, 'Jack Antonoff on what makes Taylor Swift such a special talent' (2020). Page 65 from The Conversation, 'How did Taylor Swift get so popular? She never goes out of style' (Kate Pattinson, 2023). Page 70 from Variety, 'Taylor Swift, Film Director, in Conversation With Martin McDonagh' (Ramin Setoodeh, 2022). Page 71 from The New Yorker, 'Taylor Swift's Self-Scrutiny in "Miss Americana"' (Amanda Petrusich, 2020). Page 72 from Elle, 'Taylor Swift Has No Regrets' (Tavi Gevinson, 2015). Page 73 Mail Online, 'A rebel . . . but only sometimes: Meet the four new faces of Taylor Swift as her new CoverGirl campaign is debuted' (2012). Page 74 from Be Your Own You, 'Taylor Swift Motivational Speech' (2017). Page 80 from Elle Magazine, '30 Things I Learned Before Turning 30' (Taylor Swift, 2019). Page 81 from Inc, 'Taylor Swift Says Living a Happy, Successful, and Meaningful Life Comes Down to 5 Simple Things' (Jeff Haden, 2023). Page 82 from Variety, 'Ice Spice's Red Hot Rise' (Steven Horowitz, 2023). Page 83 from People, 'Taylor Swift Says She's 'Never Been This Happy in All Aspects of My Life' During Eras Tour Stop' (2023). Page 84 from Cosmopolitan, 'Taylor Swift and Emma Stone's Super Sweet Friendship Goes Way Back' (Samantha Olson, 2024). Page 85 from US Magazine, 'Blake Lively Says BFF Taylor Swift Is 'Even Better In Real Life' While Sharing

ACKNOWLEDGEMENTS

Joyful Party Photos' (Nicole Massabrook, 2023). Page 86 from BBC News, 'Taylor Swift: Don't base your day and your happiness on social media' (2015). Page 92 from Entertainment Weekly, 'Taylor Swift's Debut Album Turns 10 - Watch Her First ET Interview!' (2016). Page 93 from Entertainment Weekly, 'Taylor Swift's Debut Album Turns 10 - Watch Her First ET Interview!' (2016). Page 94 from Inc, 'Taylor Swift Says Living a Happy, Successful, and Meaningful Life Comes Down to 5 Simple Things' (Jeff Haden, 2023). Page 95 from Elle, 'For Taylor Swift, Pop Is Personal' Taylor Swift, 2019). Page 96 from Marie Claire, 'Taylor Swift: I Started Writing Songs Because I Had No Friends' (Lisa Potter, 2013). Page 97 from People, 'Taylor Swift Says She's 'Never Been This Happy in All Aspects of My Life' During Eras Tour Stop' (2023). Page 102 from Glamour, 'Taylor Swift: Bomb-Shell in Blue Jeans' (Laurie Sandell, 2009). Page 103 from NME, 'Watch Taylor Swift give a passionate speech to mark the start of Pride Month' (Sam Moore, 2018). Page 104 from Time Magazine, '2023 Person of the Year' (Sam Lansky, 2023). Page 105 from NME, 'Watch Taylor Swift give a passionate speech to mark the start of Pride Month' (Sam Moore, 2018). Page 106 from Esquire, 'The ESQ&A: Taylor Swift' (Scott Raab, 2014). Page 112 from Taylor Swift Age 16 First National Radio Interview. Page 113 from herbsudzin, 'Taylor Swift Interview in 2007' (Herb Sudzin, 2007). Page 114 from herbsudzin, 'Taylor Swift Interview (Herb Sudzin, 2007). Page 115 from Marie Claire, 'Taylor Swift's Rise to America's Sweetheart' (Kimberly Cutter, 2010). Page 116 from Cosmopolitan, 'All the sweet details of Taylor Swift and Jack Antonoff's friendship' (Mehera Bonner, 2024). Page 117 from Taylor Swift Age 16 First National Radio Interview. Page 118 from Vulture 'Why Taylor Swift Is the Reigning Queen of Pop' (Jody Rosen, 2013).